POISONED FORESTS

Honor Head

Gareth Stevens
PUBLISHING

Please visit our website, **www.garethstevens.com**.
For a free color catalog of all our high-quality books,
call toll free 1-800-542-2595 or fax 1-877-542-2596.

Cataloging-in-Publication Data

Names: Head, Honor.
Title: Poisoned forests / Honor Head.
Description: New York : Gareth Stevens Publishing, 2019. | Series: Totally toxic
| Includes glossary and index.
Identifiers: ISBN 9781538235034 (pbk.) | ISBN 9781538235041 (library bound)
Subjects: LCSH: Forest protection--Juvenile literature.
| Forest conservation--Juvenile literature. | Forests and forestry--Juvenile literature.
Classification: LCC SD411.H43 2019 | DDC 578.73--dc23

First Edition

Published in 2019 by
Gareth Stevens Publishing
111 East 14th Street, Suite 349
New York, NY 10003

© 2019 Gareth Stevens Publishing

Produced for Gareth Stevens by Calcium
Editors: Sarah Eason and Honor Head
Designers: Paul Myerscough and Steve Mead

Photo credits: Cover: Shutterstock: Stephen Bonk; Inside: ©FSC UK/A.Chilver:
p. 41; Shutterstock: Akhenaton Images: p. 25b; Allen Paul Photography: p. 15t;
Ilya Andriyanov: p. 33b; Anticiclo: p. 28; atiger: p. 27b; Rich Carey: pp. 9, 20;
Cascade Creatives: p. 35b; ESB Professional: p. 61; Frontpage: p. 16; g215: p. 43b;
Maria Govorukhina: p. 42; guentermanaus: p. 8b; humphery: p. 18l; inewsfoto:
p. 23t; JohannesOehl: p. 10l; kakteen: p. 24b; Karine 1410: p. 7; Kletr: pp. 8, 36t;
Lisette van der Kroon: p. 21t; KucherAV: p. 5b; kudla: p. 13b; LagunaticPhoto: p. 13t;
majeczka: p. 40t; c12: p. 40b; Nada B: p. 25t; nito: p. 43t; Orla: p. 33t; Padarilhos
pp. 1, 19; Pajtica: p. 23b; Pedro Helder Pinheiro: p. 11t; pio3: p. 14; Bruce Raynor:
p. 39; Dr Morley Read: p. 11b; Ian Redding: p. 32b; Matyas Rehak: p. 17;
ShutterPNPhotography: p. 30; sittitap: p. 4b; ssguy: p. 26m; Nick Stubbs: p. 38b;
tchara: p. 37; testing: p. 27t; Unigraphoto: p. 31t; Lovelyday Vandy: p. 5t;
wandee007: p. 22; welcomia: p. 34; worldswildlifewonders: p. 12; yevgeniy11:
p. 29; Jeff Zehnder: p. 6r.

Printed in the United States of America

CPSIA compliance information: Batch #CW19GS.
For further information contact Gareth Stevens, New York, New York, at 1-800-542-2595.

CONTENTS

CHAPTER 1
TREES OF LIFE..................................4

CHAPTER 2
RAIN FORESTS 10

CHAPTER 3
DISAPPEARING TREES 18

CHAPTER 4
DIRTY AIR 26

CHAPTER 5
TREES AND WOODLANDS...............32

CHAPTER 6
MAKING THINGS RIGHT 38

BE AN ECO REPORTER! 44

GLOSSARY 46
FOR MORE INFORMATION...............47
INDEX..48

TREES OF LIFE

Forests are a crucial part of the earth's ecosystem. Trees absorb harmful carbon dioxide gases, helping to keep the air clean. One tree alone can remove 48 pounds (22 kg) of pollution from the air in a year. Through photosynthesis, trees release oxygen—which all living things need to breathe—into the air. Forests have the widest range of biodiversity on the planet. They consist of more than 10,000 different kinds of trees, and they provide food and homes to more than half a million different types of insects, mammals, birds, fish, reptiles, amphibians, and people.

Forests help regulate our climate. Whole communities of people live in some forests.

Food and Medicine

Forest trees and plants provide humans with a wide variety of food. Many plants found in forests are used to make medicines that have saved millions of lives. For example, the Madagascar periwinkle is a shrub found in tropical and subtropical forests. It is used in medicines to help cure children of a form of leukemia that once would have meant certain death. It is believed that the periwinkle has saved the lives of more than 100,000 children in the United States.

The Madagascar periwinkle is just one of many forest plants that has saved lives.

Roots and Soil

Every part of a tree is valuable for the health of our planet. Tree roots help to bind soil together, which keeps it from being washed away in heavy rains. If soil is washed away, it leaves the land bare, so that no more plants can grow. Muddy soil clogs sewers and drains, causing them to overflow and wastewater to escape. Soil that ends up in rivers and lakes pollutes the water and makes it murky, so that fish cannot see prey. The soil may suffocate the fish and their prey.

Wood from trees is used in hundreds of everyday products, including pencils and notebooks.

Forests Around the World

There are many different types of forest ecosystems, from alpine trees in frozen mountain regions to palm trees in hot tropics. Huge forests of coniferous trees, such as firs, spruce, larch, and pine, grow in North America, Europe, and Asia. Boreal or taiga forests thrive in freezing cold temperatures and icy winds. Conifers have needlelike leaves that protect them from water loss during the coldest weather. Their branches bend easily, so that they do not break under the weight of snow and ice.

Conifers provide a lot of the wood that is used in construction, as well as paper products and even products such as turpentine. Coniferous biomes absorb more carbon from the air than tropical or temperate forests, helping to keep our air clean and protecting the planet from global warming. The biggest threat to our boreal forest is from human activity, such as mining. The Amazon rain forests in South America are also under threat from mining. Mining harms the delicate ecosystem and destroys trees. Oil spills and toxic chemicals damage the food chain and pollute the air and water.

The shape of conifers allows snow to slide off easily.

Tropical trees thrive in hot, steamy places.

Four Seasons

Temperate forests thrive in regions where there are four distinct seasons, and where the summers are mild and the winters cool. The deciduous trees found here have broad leaves that drop before winter. Beetles and other insects scurry around the forest floor eating dead animals and fallen leaves. Small mammals, such as squirrels, mice, and chipmunks, feed on the fruits, seeds, and nuts that cover the forest floor. Many birds migrate to warmer countries during the winter, then return to the temperate forest to build nests and lay their eggs when the weather is warmer.

One of the world's most amazing biomes is the tropical rain forest, which is home to millions of different animal and plant species. Spiders, snakes, macaws, monkeys, eagles, frogs, jaguars, lizards, bats, caiman, sloths, river dolphins, piranha, and tapirs all live in rain forests. The rain forests are vital in helping to control climate change.

In winter, trees in temperate forests usually lose all their leaves. New leaves will grow again in the spring.

Under Threat

All the world's forests are threatened by air, water, and soil pollution from many different sources. A United Nations (UN) report predicts that the world's population will reach 8.6 billion by 2030. This means that more houses, schools, hospitals, roads, and food will be needed. Plus, developing countries are getting richer and demanding more luxury goods to buy, including goods made from desirable forest trees. A Greenpeace report stated that 72 percent of forest in Indonesia, Southeast Asia, and 15 percent of Amazon forest have already been lost forever.

Trees in this coniferous forest are being cut down and transported to processing plants and factories.

Logging and Burning

Forests are being destroyed to make everyday items such as packaging, and to provide timber for houses, furniture, and other wooden goods. Cutting down trees to be made into goods is called logging. The felled trees are cut into logs and taken to factories to be processed before they are shipped around the world. A method called slash-and-burn is used to clear forest land temporarily or permanently. If a forest is permanently cleared, it destroys habitats and leaves communities that live in the forest homeless.

Rain forest trees are cut down and burned to create farmland. This is called slash-and-burn clearing.

From Forest to Field

One of the biggest environmental problems today is the destruction of rain forests to create agricultural land on which crops—such as soybeans, cocoa beans, tea, coffee, and rubber—are grown. Another fast-growing industry is palm oil. This is a cheap oil used for cooking in developing countries and in globally used goods, such as lipstick, detergents, and ice cream. Palm trees grow quickly, and their oil is easier to produce than other oils. Palm oil production can make the corporations that fund it very rich.

Destroying forests kills wildlife, weakens the food chain, makes local communities homeless, destroys livelihoods, damages the environment, and fills the air and ground with toxic chemicals that harm people and animals.

Rain forest cleared for a palm oil plantation destroys the habitats of thousands of animals. Orangutans in Borneo and Sumatra, in Indonesia, are endangered due to loss of habitat.

CHAPTER 2
RAIN FORESTS

Rain forests are hot, wet, humid, and steamy places filled with the sounds of birds, monkeys, and other animals that live there. Rain forests are found in Central and South America, Africa, Asia, and Australia. The Amazon rain forest in South America is the biggest in the world.

Some of the animals that live in rain forest trees, such as monkeys and sloths, rarely come down to the ground; instead, they move around and raise a family in the trees. If the trees are destroyed, they will not be able to find shelter or food or move around, and they will die.

Plants called epiphytes grow high up in the trees, clinging to branches with their roots. These plants cannot survive on the ground. If the rain forest is lost, then so is all this amazing biodiversity.

This sloth and her baby spend most of their lives in rain forest trees. They eat, sleep, and feed in the trees. If their trees are cut down, they will become extinct.

Ecosystem Under Threat

The rain forest is one huge ecosystem that needs rain and sun, as well as living things to keep it healthy. Leaves, fruit, flowers and berries, dead insects, and animals all rot down to become leaf litter on the forest floor. Leaf litter is full of nutrients that trees take up through their roots to grow tall and strong. The thick spread of canopy leaves and branches keeps the forest from flooding, so that the leaf litter isn't washed away. If rain becomes toxic or the soil is polluted, this will affect the entire rain forest ecosystem.

Jaguars rest and sleep in rain forest trees. They often drag their food into the trees, away from other meat eaters.

Forest Levels

The rain forest has four main levels. At the bottom, the forest floor is where lizards, insects, snakes, and small, burrowing mammals, such as agoutis, live. Each tree has thick roots just below the surface that soak up nutrients from the ground. Very little sun shines through the trees to reach the rain forest floor.

A few feet up from the forest floor is the understory level, where animals such as leopards, jaguars, and three-toed sloths live. The level above this is called the canopy, and it is home to more than 50 percent of all plant species in the world, as well as a wide range of animals.

In rain forests, it rains every day, which means there is always fresh water for animals to drink.

Forest Food Chains

The emergent layer is at the very top of the forest. Here, trees can reach a height of more than 230 feet (70 m). The top of the rain forest is windy and very hot. Rain forests are so dense that it can take up to 10 minutes for raindrops to reach the ground.

Each level of the rain forest is linked to the one below by a food chain. Seeds and fruit that fall to the forest floor are food for small animals and insects, which are eaten by larger animals and birds, which are then eaten by even bigger animals and birds, right up to the very top of the food chain. The jaguar is a predator at the top of the food chain. It hunts birds and small mammals that feed on insects that feed on plants. The harpy eagle is another top predator that hunts in the emergent layer. It eats small monkeys, which eat the fruit and flowers that grow on trees.

Protecting the Chain

If one link in the food chain is broken, it could be catastrophic for the rest of the chain, causing death by starvation. If there is not enough food, some animals don't breed or the young die. This could eventually lead to the extinction of some species in the wild.

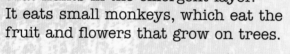

A harpy eagle sits at the very top of the rain forest trees, on the lookout for prey such as small monkeys.

Food for All

Like all forests, the rain forest also provides humans with a wide variety of food. Many tribes and communities that live in the forest depend on fish from the forest rivers. They also eat forest animals, and fruits, vegetables, and nuts from the trees. Food from rain forests is transported around the world. Avocados, oranges, cocoa beans for making chocolate, yams, plantains, and peanuts all come from the rain forests, as well as spices such as ginger, vanilla, and nutmeg.

Avocados from rain forests are one of thousands of foods transported around the globe.

Fast Food

In the past, most rain forest foods came from small farms that only needed to make enough money to support their familes or small communities. Today, with the worldwide demand for more and cheaper foods, many farmers are cutting down forest to grow trees that are not naturally found in the forest. These trees need full sun to grow quickly and are treated with pesticides. This produces toxic runoff, which pollutes the soil and waterways. The destruction of habitat and toxic pollution affects plants and animals.

Cocoa beans have been harvested in the rain forest for generations, but now big businesses are taking over the production.

Pure Air

Trees use the sun and rain to make oxygen in their leaves, which they then release into the air. All land animals need to breathe oxygen to stay alive. Trees also absorb carbon monoxide and other harmful gases, such as sulfur dioxide and ozone, from the air. In this way, trees help to keep our air clean and help to prevent dirty, suffocating smogs, which can cause breathing difficulties for many people. In 2012, the World Health Organization (WHO) estimated that 3.7 million premature deaths were caused by outdoor air pollution. In the city of Nanjing, China, which has some of the world's most poisonous air, apartment buildings are being designed with trees planted at every level, in an attempt to clean the polluted air and make the surroundings pleasant for everyone.

In Central Park, people can relax and enjoy nature. The trees also help keep the air clean.

Climate Control

Trees play a major role in helping to control our weather. Their leaves help keep our air cool through a process called evapotranspiration. A tree draws up water through its roots, so that it can grow and stay healthy. This process is called transpiration. The water evaporates and is released into the air as a vapor or gas through the leaves. This keeps our air cool and moist. Trees also provide us with shade in summer, helping to keep us cool. Leaves filter harmful particles from the air, such as dust and carbon dioxide.

A large oak tree can transpire 40,000 gallons (151,400 liters) of water into the atmosphere in one year.

WHO'S TO BLAME? THE TOXIC TRUTH

Schweighofer is a company based in Austria, Europe. It is controlled by one of the wealthiest families in that country. The company is allegedly encouraging the illegal logging of trees in untouched forests in Romania, in Europe. Reports by the Environmental Investigation Agency (EIA) claim that the company is buying huge amounts of wood that has been illegally chopped down from these forests. The company encourages further deforestation by offering to pay bonuses for more wood. The destruction of this forest threatens the livelihood of local communities, the environment, and the wildlife that lives there. But who is to blame: Schweighofer for allegedly buying illegal wood; the logging companies for chopping down the trees; or the Romanian government for not having stricter controls on deforestation? Are they all partly to blame? Debate arguments "for and against" the buyers, loggers, and government

Worldwide Wind

Teleconnections means "connection at a distance," and it is a term used to describe how wind patterns connect different parts of the world. It is believed that because of teleconnections, deforestation in one part of the world can have an impact on the other side of the planet. A huge amount of rain forest destruction can cause the air to become dryer and warmer, and this warm air can be carried to other parts of the world. This results in less rainfall and possible drought in agricultural areas.

Less rainfall affects crops and means a shortage of food for local people or an increase in food prices globally. Scientists believe that complete deforestation of the Amazon rain forest would affect agriculture in the United States. Drought can also reduce the water available for drinking and other household activities.

Huge areas of land around the world are being deforested. The loss of all these trees could have a damaging effect on agriculture around the world.

Forests are being destroyed so that huge dams, such as this one in Brazil, South America, can be built to power ever-growing cities.

Building Dams

As well as clearing forests for farming, mining, and other activities, trees are also cleared to build massive hydropower projects, such as dams. The Balbina Dam in Brazil, South America, was first started in 1985. To build the dam, large areas of the rain forest were flooded, creating thousands of small "islands" of forest. This was a disaster for local people and the environment. It also affected wildlife by destroying and fragmenting their habitat. It is estimated that more than 70 percent of the animal populations stranded on the "islands" have now become extinct.

Double Disaster

Brazil relies on hydropower for its electricity. Many people agree that hydropower can be a clean and effective way to generate electricity. However, scientists have also discovered that forests that have been covered in water may be releasing large amounts of deadly methane gas into the air, adding to the greenhouse effect. Up to 61 new dams are to be built in Brazil over the next few years, and their impact could be an environmental disaster. Not only are the dams destroying forest that can help control greenhouse gases, but they are also contributing to them—a double disaster for the world's climates.

CHAPTER 3

DISAPPEARING TREES

Furniture made from mahogany, a valuable rain forest wood, is on sale at a special fair in China.

Most of our forests have been growing for thousands of years, but it takes only a few hours to destroy whole areas forever. The deliberate destruction of forests is called deforestation. This is happening around the world, especially in the Amazon rain forest.

Most rain forest deforestation is illegal, but local governments either can't or won't do anything about it. The destruction of rain forest is usually done by powerful international companies that make huge profits from farming the land or from selling valuable rain forest wood.

Some of the most beautiful wood in the world comes from rain forests. These are hardwoods, such as teak, mahogany, ebony, and rosewood. Furniture, ornaments, and other products made from these woods can be sold for a lot of money in some countries where there is a high demand for them.

Fire, Fire

As populations increase, forests are also destroyed to build towns. This destruction has several damaging effects. Without tree roots to hold the soil together, it is washed away into rivers and streams, which can suffocate fish. Chemical runoff from construction works seeps into the soil and waterways and, eventually, the ocean.

One of the main ways that forests are destroyed is by deliberately setting them on fire. This kills and injures animals, and drives them out of their habitat, leaving them homeless and exposed. Burning trees may also release dangerous toxins into the air that can be harmful to people living nearby. Constant exposure to wood smoke can cause skin disease, asthma, bronchitis, and other breathing problems to humans.

Peat Forests

Peat swamp forests are tropical forests where it is so wet that the ground is constantly waterlogged. Dead leaves and wood that fall to the ground don't fully decompose but break down into a layer of thick, sludgy mud called peat. Peat forests absorb huge amounts of harmful carbon gas from the air. There are peat forests and swamps around the world, but the largest are in Indonesia and Borneo, in Southest Asia, where they are being illegally burned to create deforested land. The trees burn down quickly, but the peat smolders slowly, releasing dangerous carbon gas into the air.

Burning is a fast way to clear forest land. The world's rain forests are disappearing at a rate of 6,000 acres (2,428 ha) per hour.

Illegal Logging

One of the main causes of deforestation is logging. Trees are cut down, and their wood is sold to be made into products such as furniture or construction materials. Or, the wood is processed into paper that is used for goods such as toilet paper, packaging, books, and newspapers. Much of the logging that happens in tropical rain forests is illegal, and it is threatening areas from the Amazon, in South America, to Russia, in Eastern Europe.

Before logging can begin, roads are cut through forests, disturbing wildlife and destroying habitats. If local communities object, they are often bullied or threatened into staying quiet and accepting what is happening. Sometimes, people are killed. Next, the loggers arrive. They are usually migrant workers from outside local communities; they are paid well and have no interest in the forest environment or wildlife. Trees are chopped down, cut into logs, stacked on trucks, and taken to sawmills. Some local communities have gained financially from the demand for timber, but usually, the profit goes to the powerful logging companies.

A bulldozer crashes through the rain forest in Borneo, in Asia, to make a road for loggers.

In this Borneo rain forest, trees have been destroyed and turned into logs. They will be taken to sawmills and factories.

WHO'S TO BLAME? THE TOXIC TRUTH

Indonesia, in Southeast Asia, has huge swathes of swamp forests where ramin trees grow. These trees are a protected species. The forest is also home to the endangered Sumatran tiger. The company Asia Pulp & Paper (APP), based in Indonesia, is one of the world's largest pulp, packaging, and paper companies, and it has been accused of illegally clearing vast areas of the swamp forest. By doing this, the company can supply paper at a much cheaper rate than their competitors.

A report by Friends of the Earth claimed that more than 300 banks and financial institutions globally helped to finance APP. Much of the end product is sold to paper merchants and retailers, who then sell the paper on to branded companies. APP denies any wrongdoing. In a situation like this, who is to blame: the government, for not enforcing local logging laws; the people who finance big companies; the big companies wanting higher profits; or the smaller retailers looking for cheaper alternatives? What could be done to stop this cycle?

Cattle and Crops

Land cleared for farming is another big threat to the world's forests. Forest is cleared to make land available for cattle ranches, where cows are raised to provide the increasing amount of beef that is eaten around the world, especially in fast-food hamburger restaurants. Clearing the forests destroys trees that soak up carbon dioxide. Cattle release toxic fumes, such as methane, into the air. Runoff animal waste pollutes the soil and waterways.

Palm Oil Pollution

Palm oil is in hundreds of everyday products, from soaps to ice cream. Plantations of oil palms are now replacing forests in Asia and West Africa, and most of the world's oil palm plantations are found in Malaysia and Indonesia, in Southeast Asia. As with all deforestation, clearing land for oil palm trees devastates wildlife by destroying habitats, and it displaces local people. Fires from forest clearance fill the air with toxic smoke, which causes unhealthy smogs. The thinking is that palm oil will help reduce greenhouse gases by creating biofuels, which are better for the environment. But the destruction of forests and the burning of peatlands release more carbon into the air than burning fossil fuels.

Palm oil trees produce cheap cooking oil, and when the oil is added to other foods, it increases their shelf life.

Soybean Plantations

It's not just palm trees that require cleared forest land. Soybean crops are also responsible for forests being cleared. Soybeans are a cheap form of protein used in animal feed on farms, some pet foods, as a meat substitute in packaged meals, and in condiments and vegetable oil. The United States, and Brazil and Argentina, in South America, grow most of the world's soybean crops. China, in Asia, is the world's biggest soybean importer.

Soybeans can be grown in both temperate and tropical regions. As well as destroying forests that help to keep our planet healthy, growing soybeans on such a large scale requires huge amounts of pesticides, herbicides, and fertilizers. These contaminate the soil and waterways around the farms with toxic chemicals that can harm humans and animals.

Soybeans are used to make soy sauce, used a lot in Asian food.

Fertilizers and pesticides that are used to make soybean crops grow fast are adding to land and water pollution.

WHO'S TO BLAME?
THE TOXIC TRUTH

Palm oil brings Indonesia and Malaysia staggering profits of about $40 billion a year. But the price is the destruction of forest that cannot be replaced, dead animals, environmental disaster, toxic air with the fumes from fires, and the release of large amounts of carbon dioxide into the atmosphere, which adds to global warming. Permits to destroy the forests are often given even on protected land, as the profits are so great. Many large global brands have stopped using palm oil in their products, or they are only buying the oil from traceable and sustainable sources, but many more are not, and the destruction and devastation continues. Can we blame governments, manufacturers, or consumers for the boom in the demand for palm oil? What solutions can you think of to stop the devastation caused by palm oil crops?

Precious Metals

Mining for precious metals, such as gold, copper, and silver, destroys forests around the world. Mining in the Amazon rain forest in South Ameria is often done illegally or in agreement with corrupt government officials. Miners blast a huge hole in riverbanks and dig craters in forest clearings. They use pressurized water to wash away the earth. Next, they sieve the soil with deadly poisons, such as cyanide and mercury, that bind with any gold pieces.

Toxic sediment from the blasting and washing seeps into rivers, suffocating fish and damaging river plants and animals. The mercury and cyanide are washed into the soil and rivers, contaminating the water, harming wildlife, and poisoning drinking water. Water can remain poisoned for a long time, sometimes forever.

Wastewater from gold mining in Guyana, South America, floods into the forest and contaminates the ground.

Killing for Coltan

In the forests of the Congo Basin in Central Africa, a rare mineral called coltan is being mined. When coltan is refined, it becomes heat resistant and can hold a high electric charge. It is now a vital element in circuit boards used for devices such as cell phones and computers.

Coltan mining is generally illegal and unregulated, and it is run by militia–style groups that threaten and kill local people who get in their way. The miners blast the forest and pollute the environment with toxic chemicals and harmful mining runoff. Our constant demand for new faster and better digital devices means that the price for coltan stays high. As consumers, we can help this situation by not replacing our devices so often and making sure we donate our old ones to charities.

In mining for coltan in the Congo, Africa, chemicals are mixed with soil to find the metal. The toxic runoff poisons the whole environment.

Coltan is used in nearly every electronic device that we use, including cell phones, but mining for coltan is causing environmental devastation in some countries.

CHAPTER 4
DIRTY AIR

Each day, our air is filled with dirt, dust, and toxic gases that cause air pollution. Air pollution is anything in the air that has a damaging effect on people, wildlife, or the environment. One of the worst pollutants is carbon dioxide, which joins other gases—such as methane, nitrous oxide, and ozone—to make up the greenhouse gases.

When heat from the sun reaches Earth, it is absorbed by land and water. Then, energy bounces back into the atmosphere in the form of infrared rays. The greenhouse gases trap these rays to keep our planet warm. Without greenhouse gases, the earth would be a frozen wasteland without any life forms. However, too many gases act like a greenhouse and keep the infrared rays from leaving the earth. This is causing the earth's temperature to warm up too much and is causing climate change, which affects the whole planet.

Air pollution is one of the most serious problems our planet faces. This smoke from burning coal contains toxic carbon dioxide.

Too Much Carbon

The main source of carbon dioxide is from burning fossil fuels, such as oil, gas, and coal. These are used in our homes, schools, in factories, and in large industrial sites to generate electricity. Fossil fuels are also used in automobiles, trucks, and planes.

Many power plants around the world still use coal to generate power for electricity. Huge furnaces burn the coal and produce smoke that is pumped into the air. Exhaust fumes from road traffic and airplanes also release carbon dioxide into the air. Factories that use coal, gas, or wood—and homes that burn coal and wood for heat—all contribute to the toxic chemicals in our air.

Some countries are trying to control the amount of carbon dioxide that is released into the air. In 2016, leaders from 118 nations met in Paris to sign an agreement (called the Paris Agreement) to try to control global climate change.

Heavy traffic in Bejing, China, pours toxic exhaust fumes into the air.

A hazy, dirty smog hangs over the city of Shanghai, China. Many people wear face masks when they go out.

Acid rain has killed this forest in Germany, in Europe.

Acid Rain

When coal and gas are burned, they release sulfur, which reacts with the air to create sulfur dioxide, a deadly toxin. The sulfur dioxide reacts with vapor in the clouds and falls to the ground as acid rain or mist. This toxic rain damages trees and makes them weak, and it harms the leaves, so that they can't turn sunlight into food. Acid rain drips into the soil around trees and dissolves essential nutrients, such as potassium and calcium that trees need to grow and stay strong. Toxins in the soil from acid rain are taken up through the roots and poison the trees. When trees are weak, they can be attacked by diseases and insects that may kill them. Also they are unable to survive extremes of weather such as heat and cold. Other plants and wildlife also suffer, so the whole forest ecosystem is seriously damaged.

Regulations

Acid rain also gets into waterways, lakes, and rivers, and eventually reaches the ocean, where it kills fish and other wildlife. Power plants in Europe and North America have regulations to control how much sulfur dioxide is released, and they have special filters in chimneys. Many countries also regulate how much sulfur can be used in car fuel. However, many other countries don't have these rules, and acid rain is threatening local forests. Acid rain has badly damaged conifer forests in North America, Central Europe, and Scandinavia, in northwestern Europe.

Trash Mountains

Landfills are where all our trash goes. These gigantic piles of garbage rot down and produce harmful gases, such as ammonia, methane, sulfide, and carbon dioxide. Landfill gases generally peak after five to seven years, but they can continue to produce gas for more than 50 years. Garbage that is incinerated or burned releases harmful toxins and black, choking smoke into the air. This gets into the atmosphere as rain and dust, and affects trees, humans, and wildlife.

Landfill sites release gases into the air, and 98 percent of these gases can be methane and carbon dioxide.

E-Waste: Dangerous and Illegal

Electronic waste, known as e-waste, refers to anything electric or electronic, such as printers, cell phones, computers, televisions, and game consoles. As we buy more and more electronic equipment and demand to update and upgrade it on a regular basis, so tons more e-waste is being created.

More than 40 million tons of electronic equipment is thrown away every year. It is difficult and expensive to dispose of safely, so almost 90 percent of e-waste is being illegally dumped, most of it in developing countries. Many of these countries don't have laws that regulate how e-waste should be disposed of safely. For example, wires are often burned to get to the valuable copper inside. The burning releases hydrocarbons into the air. Chemicals used to strip computer chips of their gold plating release toxins into the air and into the soil, and these poisons can harm the trees.

Africa now has electronic graveyards. Electronic waste is exported from the West to countries such as Nigeria and Ghana in Africa.

Toxic Fumes

In some places, old electronic waste is tossed onto an open fire to burn away nonvaluable metals and melt plastic wire coverings. This releases harmful chemicals into the air—some are known to cause cancer—that create noxious fumes and dangerous dust. The deadly smog creates health problems for the local population and wildlife, contaminating waterways and drinking water, and damaging trees.

Wires from the inside of e-waste are burned to get to the copper inside, which is then sold.

WHO'S TO BLAME? THE TOXIC TRUTH

In Ghana, Africa, on a pile of e-waste, Mohammed is working. He's 10 years old and is looking for copper wire to sell. He's been working on the dump site since his mother died, and he needs the dimes he makes to buy food. The dump is dangerous. He can cut himself on sharp metal, and the cuts can become infected. He has headaches caused by the toxic fumes. The deadly chemicals he breathes in could lead to lung and breathing problems. The fumes being released into the air can create dangerous smogs that will affect human health, animals, and the environment.

Countries send old, broken electronic items, such as televisions and washing machines, to developing countries, claiming that they work and can be sold as cheap secondhand goods. The items don't work and end up in these dumps. Is this fair? Why should we dump our broken and dangerous e-waste in another country? Who's to blame—our governments or the countries that take the e-waste? How can we keep this from happening?

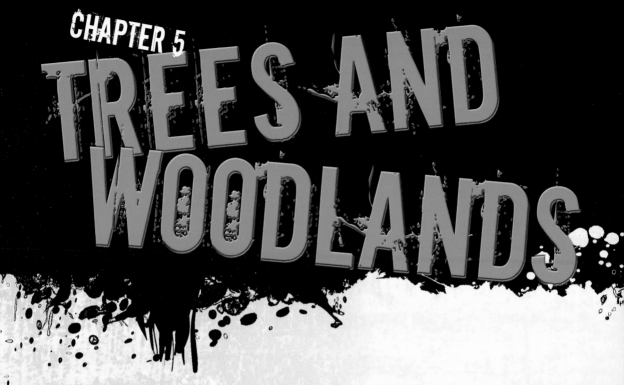

CHAPTER 5
TREES AND WOODLANDS

Woodlands are vital to the environment for many reasons. They are great for outdoor activities, such as walking, camping, bird-watching, and fishing in the woodland streams. Smaller areas of woodland are usually a part of a previously much larger woodland that may have been cut down to make way for roads, housing, or farming. Woodlands are home to a wide range of biodiversity, from fungi that grow in rotting leaves, to birds that nest in the branches of trees and small animals that scurry around the woodland floor. Woodland trees are an important source of food for birds and animals all year round, especially during the fall and winter, when they stock up on nuts and berries and feed on small insects.

Woodlands are peaceful, beautiful places for people to visit, and they provide food and shelter for animals.

We Need Trees

Trees absorb pollution from the air, such as dust, pollen, and toxins. Research has shown that tree-lined streets can reduce the levels of asthma in children and help reduce breathing problems caused by pollution in adults. Having access to trees and woodland can also relieve stress and anxiety and improve our mental health.

Belowground, the tree's root system feeds the tree and filters out toxins that contaminate the air.

Waterways

Trees help protect water habitats such as lakes and rivers. The roots of trees that line rivers and lakes help filter out harmful fertilizer, pesticide, and chemical runoff from farms, factories, and homes. They can also trap dirt and oil from road runoff. Research has shown that tree roots help to maintain healthy soil, which is good for the trees, insects, lizards, and other animals that are part of the food chain.

In areas with soil that contains sand, peat, and heavy clay, trees act as a barrier to keep the soil from being washed away into rivers by wind and rain, and so keep them free from toxins. Much of the water we get from our faucets begins in woodland streams and lakes.

Most of our drinking water comes from local freshwater sources. Trees help keep this water safe to drink.

Invisible Giants

California has some of the most stunning forests in the United States, such as Sequoia National Park, which is home to the world's largest trees. Sadly, you can't always see them because they are covered in a low-lying toxic haze made up of sulfates, nitrates, dust, and smoke. The park is above the San Joaquin Valley, which is a big area for farming and industry. The farms, dairies, and factories in the valley produce air that is polluted with chemicals from fertilizers and pesticides, smoke from factories, and smog from constant road traffic. The wind carries the polluted air up the valley, where it is trapped in the forest and hangs above the trees as a brown haze. The giant sequoia trees don't seem to be affected, but ozone in the smog can affect the growth of young trees. The needles on pine trees turn yellow and drop off.

Checking the Air

The U.S. Environmental Protection Agency (EPA) regularly monitors the air quality in the parks and has found that the pollution levels are often unhealthy or risky for people with breathing problems, such as children with asthma. Government agencies are changing air quality laws to help reduce the pollution levels, and in 2018, the air quality had improved, but it is an ongoing battle.

Giant sequoia trees reach up into the sky. Sequoia National Park, California, is home to some of the largest and oldest trees on Earth.

WHO'S TO BLAME? THE TOXIC TRUTH

People are planting illegal marijuana farms deep in the forests in California. The growers bulldoze land to create roads and farm areas. They use a highly toxic rodenticide to keep rats away from the plants. This kills the rats slowly and stays in the animals' bodies for days, spreading through the food chain. Runoff from the rodenticide gets into the soil and waterways, and toxic silt from the farms is washed into rivers and streams. Water used to grow the crop is drying out streams and rivers, causing drought .

Most long-term marijuana growers farm responsibly and claim that "rogue" farmers are to blame. So, who's really to blame, and what can be done about it? Is it up to the police to hunt down rogue farmers? What can responsible farmers do? Should regulations governing growing marijuana be tightened up?

The U.S. Forest Service (USFS) has reported 67 illegal sites growing marijuana in 20 states.

A green energy factory is producing biogas, an energy source made from garbage from landfill sites.

Deadly Duo

Woodland trees can be seriously harmed by toxins such as nitrogen and sulfur. Nitrogen is a fertilizer, and a certain amount is good for trees and other plants, since it helps them to grow. However, too much nitrogen from farmland runoff or air pollution can harm an entire woodland ecosystem because it encourages other species of plants to grow that upset the woodland balance. Nitrogen and other toxins—such as sulfur, which has a high level of acidity—can also affect nutrients in the soil, which in turn affects the growth and health of trees.

Alternatives to Fossil Fuels

Nitrogen and other harmful toxins are produced by fossil fuels. Many companies are now looking for alternative sources of fuel to help slow down or stop the toxic affect of fossil fuels in our environment. Biomass fuels are one idea. Biomass means "natural materials," such as dead plants, yard waste, and crops. These materials are processed and turned into tiny pellets that are used to heat homes and industry. This heat also creates energy that can be used to give us electricity and to power machines in factories. Biomass fuels include wood. Burning wood can help to save forests if new, fast-growing trees are planted and managed correctly. Burning biomass fuel creates heat that we can use, but it means there is less toxic waste in our air.

Top Trash

When the garbage in landfill sites decays and rots down, it releases a gas called biogas. When biogas is burned, it releases far less toxic carbon dioxide into the air than fossil fuels. Animal manure and human waste can also be turned into biogas, which can be used as a fuel for road vehicles. Biofuels are being considered as possible alternatives to power trains in India, the United States, the United Kingdom, Sweden in northern Europe, and other countries. The use of biofuels may help reduce the amount of toxic chemicals in the air.

These biomass wood pellets have been made from fast-growing coniferous trees.

CHAPTER 6

MAKING THINGS RIGHT

As the world's population grows, more forest is turned into farms for food. More forests are destroyed for wood for construction of towns and cities. As more people want more goods, such as furniture, more factories will use more fossil fuels to produce these goods. All this increases the amount of toxic waste from farming, factories, transportation, garbage dumps, and e-waste. Factories producing more goods create more heat. There are millions more vehicles on the roads and planes in the sky, and larger cattle ranches providing meat for food. All this leads to increased global warming. Even an increase of a couple of degrees can have a huge impact on every living thing on the planet.

Chimneys at a power plant in Poland, in Europe, pump dirty smoke into the air.

Long-Term Disaster

Global warming affects weather patterns and temperatures around the world. It is causing the polar ice caps to melt, which will cause sea levels to rise. Less ice is a threat to polar bears that use it to find seals, their main source of food. Rising sea levels may flood villages and towns, making people homeless. Coral reefs are being bleached and are dying.

Dead Forests

In the vast pine forests that stretch from the Yukon Territory in Canada to southern California and New Mexico, global warming has had a disastrous effect on the trees. Pine trees are home to a small insect called a pine beetle. Usually, the pine beetles and pine trees live together without too much harm, but as a result of warmer temperatures, the pine beetle is laying more larvae that eats away at the inside of the trees, killing vast areas of pine forest.

The warmer climate also means the trees don't get enough water, so they don't have the energy to fight off attacks by the larvae. When trees die, the whole forest food chain is affected, from brown bears who eat the berries, to birds who store the seeds for winter. The trees become a ghost forest, and the soil is washed away. The whole ecosystem is damaged.

The inside of this fallen pine tree shows how the pine beetle has eaten up the tree trunk.

Renewable Energy Now!

Governments, farmers, businesses, and industries in all countries need to act to help reduce the amount of toxins contaminating our air and water and damaging our trees. There are many ways this can be tackled. Industries that use fossil fuels could investigate the possibility of using renewable energy sources. Fossil fuels will not be able to provide us with energy forever, so experts are looking at other ways of obtaining energy that are more sustainable and less of a threat to the environment.

Renewable energy made from wood, unwanted farm crops, and garbage is one form of energy that can be developed. Other renewable sources include: solar energy from the sun; wind power harnessed from wind turbines; hydropower harnessed from lake and river water; and wave power from the oceans. Geothermal energy is made from hot rocks just under the surface of the ground.

Power made from solar panels can be used by homes and industries. The panels trap heat from the sun.

Wind turns the blades at the top of the wind turbines to generate electricity. Turbines are placed in the sea or in fields where there is plenty of wind.

Legal Responsibility

Destroying forests creates an increasingly toxic environment for everyone. In countries where logging, deforestation, and mining are widespread, governments can pass laws to make sure that such activities are carried out legally and safely, and with respect for the wildlife, local people, and the environment. However, in many countries, the government or local authorities are corrupt and accept bribes to allow illegal work to continue. In some places, such as in the dense rain forests, it is almost impossible to control or police the activities of illegal operations.

Industry Awareness

Companies that buy oil products, precious metals, paper products, packaging, wood products, and so on should make sure they know the supply chain and check that the environment, wildlife, and humans have not been illegally harmed at any stage. The Forest Stewardship Council® (FSC®) is an international organization that helps care for forests and the people and animals who call them home. You can help care for forests by looking for the FSC® logo when you buy anything made from wood, cardboard, paper, or other forest-based materials.

The FSC® makes sure that forests are treated in a responsible way. Look out for the FSC® logo.

Cutting Back

Providing enough food for the world's ever-increasing population is always going to be a huge environmental issue. It is a problem that affects forests directly when they are cut down for farming, and indirectly when they are being polluted by agricultural chemicals. Farmers use huge amounts of pesticides, herbicides, fertilizers, and other chemicals to help them produce enough food for growing demands.

Vast cattle farms are responsible for deforestation, and cattle release greenhouse gases into the atmosphere. However, although we put pressure on farmers to produce more and cheaper food, there is a huge amount of food waste in most developed countries. On average, an American student is responsible for wasting 67 pounds (30 kg) of lunch food every school year, and overall, 40 percent of all food bought is thrown away in the United States each year. Wasted food comes from homes, schools, supermarkets, restaurants, hospitals, and cafes, and it usually ends up in landfill, adding to the toxins in our environment.

A higher demand for meat and meat products means that huge cattle ranches are taking up a lot of land that was once forest.

Perfect Food Only

Some food is wasted before it even reaches the consumer. Farmers often plant too many crops, in case some are damaged by disease or bad weather. Some fruit and vegetables are left unpicked because they are not the right shape or color, or because there aren't enough people to pick them. Consumers have high expectations of how food should look, and huge amounts of food can be are thrown away by farmers because it doesn't look right. In developed countries, one family can throw away between 14 and 25 percent of the food it buys. This is because food is so readily available and, mostly, cheap enough to waste. Also, there is often confusion between "sell-by" and "use-by" dates.

Ways to Improve

Farmers around the world need to consider using fewer chemicals to grow their food. As consumers, we should question why we force farmers to use chemicals to create perfect-looking fruit and vegetables. Why can't we accept food that looks less than perfect? Packaging is another issue. Plastic that can't be recycled is still widely used for food, and prepared meals come in a lot of packaging that ends up in landfill sites.

Farmers, supermarkets, restaurants, and households throw away vast amounts of food every day.

BE AN ECO REPORTER!

Trees are destroyed to provide us with a variety of everyday items, such as paper and packaging. But do we need all this packaging? Research and report it!

 The Toxic Facts

Choose an item that you have seen or bought recently that had cardboard or paper packaging. This could be anything from a sandwich to a pair of shoes.

- Explain why you think this item needs to be packaged. If you don't think it needs any packaging, explain why.

- Is all the packaging recyclable? Give a rough percentage of how much is recyclable and how much isn't.

- If it has any packaging that is nonrecyclable, how could you replace this packaging to make it all recyclable?

- At every stage of the making of an item, from the raw material it comes from (such as a tree) to manufacturing and transportation stages, carbon gas is released into the air. This is called the carbon footprint of the product.

- Investigate the carbon footprint of your item, from the raw material to the store where you bought it. Where is it from, how has it been processed or manufactured, and has it been transported a long distance? What else adds to its carbon footprint?

- Research what toxic chemicals have been released into the environment in the process of making your item and transporting it to the store.

 Report the Toxic Truth

Now, write a report about your findings. Send it to the manufacturer of the item.

- Explain how the product has polluted the environment. Give some facts and figures to back up your findings.

- If the product has nonrecyclable packaging, give the manufacturer ideas for alternative recyclable packaging. Show your ideas in a diagram with labels and captions.

- If you think the item doesn't need any packaging, explain to the manufacturer why.

- If you manufactured this product, how would you make the manufacturing process less harmful to the environment? What steps would you change?

SPREAD THE WORD

Remember, we all have a responsibility to protect our forests. Tell your family and friends what you have learned about poisoned forests and what they can all do to help protect these precious ecosystems.

GLOSSARY

biodiversity The variety and amount of animal and plant life in a habitat.

bleached Turned white. When a coral reef is bleached, it turns white and dies.

boreal Trees and forests found in colder, northern areas, such as Canada, Alaska, Sweden, Finland, and Russia. These forests are also known as taiga, a Russian word.

condiments Flavorings such as sauces added to food.

coniferous Trees that have needlelike leaves and stay green all year round.

corrupt Someone who does something illegal or dishonest, usually for money or power.

deciduous A tree that loses its leaves in the winter and then grows new ones in the spring.

decompose When dead matter, such as leaves or animals, rots away or decays in the ground.

ecosystem Living and nonliving things that work together in the environment, such as the sun, rain, and plants.

extinct A plant or animal that has died out, especially in the wild.

humid Hot and steamy.

leukemia A serious illness that affects the blood and can cause severe sickness and possibly death.

militia Armed groups that often act illegally, for themselves or for a government or person for pay.

photosynthesis The process used by trees and other plants to create food for themselves from sunlight through their leaves.

renewable Something that can be renewed. Coal and gas will eventually be used up, so they are not renewable. We will always have the sun, wind, and rain, so these are renewable sources.

runoff Water that is waste or left over from human activity in fields, roads, cities, and towns—such as sewage water from homes and fertilizer from farms.

soybeans Beans widely used around the world as a meat substitute and in flavorings. Soybeans are a good source of protein.

subtropical Close to the tropics, where summers are warm or hot and winters are mild.

supply chain The people, companies, and activities involved in making a product, all the way up to the consumer buying it. A supply chain for a wooden chair might be tree logger, sawmill, factory, ship transportation, road transportation, store, and, finally, the consumer.

sustainable Something that can be maintained at a certain level without harming the environment. Sustainable forests replace trees at the same rate they are cut down.

FOR MORE INFORMATION

Books

Cohn, Jessica. *Hand to Earth: Saving the Environment*. Huntington Beach, CA: Teacher Created Materials, 2013.

Kirk, Ellen. *Human Footprint: Everything You Will Eat, Use, Wear, Buy, and Throw Out in Your Lifetime*. Washington, D.C.: National Geographic Children's Books, 2011.

Littlewood, Antonia, and Peter Littlewood. *Rain Forest Destruction* (Mapping Global Issues). Mankato, MN: Smart Apple Media, 2012.

Mihaly, Christy. *California's Redwood Forests* (Natural Wonders of the World). Mendota Heights, MN: Focus Readers, 2018.

Websites

fs.fed.us
Find out about forest management, forest threats, wildlife, and much more from the U.S. Forest Service.

kidsagainstpalmoil.org
Discover how to help keep the forests from being destroyed for palm oil plantations on this informative site.

www.npca.org
Read about the many environmental issues surrounding America's forests at the National Parks Conservation Association site.

www.worldwildlife.org/habitats/forest-habitat
Learn more about why trees and forests are important to all living things and the threats they face.

Publisher's note to educators and parents: Our editors have carefully reviewed these websites to ensure that they are suitable for students. Many websites change frequently, however, and we cannot guarantee that a site's future contents will continue to meet our high standards of quality and educational value. Be advised that students should be closely supervised whenever they access the Internet.

INDEX

acid rain 28, 29
agricultural chemicals 42
agriculture 16
air pollution 14, 26, 36
Amazon 6, 8, 10, 16, 18, 20, 24

biodiversity 4, 10, 32
biogas 36, 37
biomass 37
boreal forest 6

carbon dioxide 4, 15, 22, 24, 26, 27, 29, 37
carbon footprint 44, 45
cell phones 25, 30
climate change 7, 26, 27
Coltan mining 25
conifers 6

deciduous trees 7
deforestation 15, 16, 18, 20, 22, 41, 42

ecosystem 4, 6, 11, 28, 36, 39
electricity 17, 27, 37, 40
electronic graveyards 30
environment 9, 15, 17, 20, 22, 25, 26, 31, 32, 37, 40, 41, 42, 45
evapotranspiration 15
e-waste 30, 31, 38
exhaust fumes 27

farmers 13, 35, 40, 42, 43
fertilizers 23, 34, 42
food waste 42
Forest Stewardship Council® (FSC®) 41
fossil fuels 22, 27, 37, 38, 40
Friends of the Earth 21

geothermal energy 40
global warming 6, 24, 38, 39
gold mining 24
green energy 36
Greenpeace 8

habitat 9, 13, 17, 19
hardwoods 18
herbicides 23, 42
hydropower 17, 40

industries 40
infrared rays 26

landfill sites 29
leaf litter 11

Madagascar periwinkle 5
manufacturing 44, 45
marijuana farms 35
methane 17, 22, 26, 29
mining 6, 17, 24, 25, 41

nonrecyclable packaging 45

Paris Agreement 27
peat forests 19
pesticides 13, 23, 34, 42
photosynthesis 4
plantations 22
power plants 27

rain forests 6, 7, 9, 11, 13, 18, 19, 20, 41
renewable energy 40
runoff 13, 19, 25, 33, 36

slash-and-burn 8
smog 27, 31, 34
solar energy 40
soybeans 9, 23

teleconnections 16
temperate forests 6, 7
toxic fumes 22, 31
toxic sediment 24
transpiration 15

United Nations (UN) 8
U.S. Environmental Protection Agency (EPA) 34
U.S. Forest Service (USFS) 35

wastewater 5
wind power 40
woodland 32, 33, 36